EDWARD LEAR'S
Non–
sense

Illustrated by
JAMES WINES

RIZZOLI
NEW YORK

First published in the United States of America in 1994
by RIZZOLI INTERNATIONAL PUBLICATIONS, INC.
300 Park Avenue South, New York, New York 10010

Library of Congress Cataloging-in-Publication Data

Lear, Edward, 1812-1888.
       Edward Lear's nonsense / illustrated by James Wines.
       p.   cm.
Summary: An illustrated collection of Lear's nonsense
verse with afterwords about the author and the artist.
      ISBN: 0-8478-1682-6
1. Children's poetry, English. 2. Nonsense verses. English.
[1. Nonsense verses. 2. Humorous poetry.
3. Limericks. 4. English poetry.]
I. Wines, James, 1932- ill.   II. Title.
      PR4879.L2A6   1994
      821'.8—dc20   93-20461

Edited by Kimberly Harbour
Designed by Lisa Mangano

Jacket illustration by James Wines
Printed and bound in Singapore

Contents

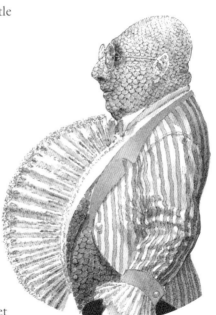

There was an Old Man
of Coblenz,

The length of whose legs was immense;

He went with one prance

From Turkey to France,

That surprising Old Man of Coblenz.

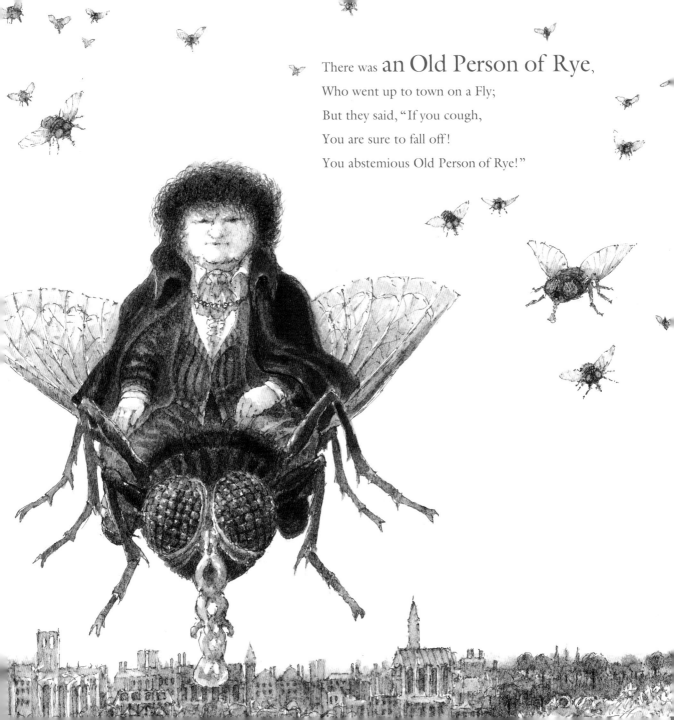

There was **an Old Person of Rye**,

Who went up to town on a Fly;

But they said, "If you cough,

You are sure to fall off!

You abstemious Old Person of Rye!"

There was **an Old Person of Brigg**,

Who purchased no end of a Wig;

So that only his Nose

And the end of his Toes

Could be seen when he walked about Brigg.

There was **an Old Person
of Sheen**,

Whose expression was calm and serene;

He sat in the water,

And drank bottled porter,

That placid Old Person of Sheen.

There was **a Young Lady of Firle**,

Whose Hair was addicted to curl;

It curled up a Tree,

And all over the Sea,

That expansive Young Lady of Firle.

There was **an Old Person of Ems**,

Who casually fell in the Thames;

And when he was found

They said he was drowned,

That unlucky Old Person of Ems.

There was **an Old Lady of Chertsey**,
Who made a remarkable curtsey;
She twisted round and round,
Til she sank underground,
Which distressed all the people of Chertsey.

There was **an Old Man with a beard**,
Who said, "It is just as I feared!—
Two Owls and a Hen,
Four Larks and a Wren,
Have all built their nests in my beard!"

There was **an Old Man in a Tree**,

Whose Whiskers were lovely to see;

But the Birds of the Air

Pluck'd them perfectly bare,

To make themselves Nests in that Tree.

There was **an Old Person of Dutton,**

Whose head was as small as a button,

So, to make it look big,

He purchased a wig,

And rapidly rushed about Dutton.

There was **an Old Man of Blackheath**,

Whose head was adorned with a Wreath,

Of lobsters and spice,

Pickled onions and mice,

That uncommon Old Man of Blackheath.

There was **an Old Person of Bude**,
Whose deportment was vicious and crude;
He wore a large Ruff
Of pale straw-colored stuff,
Which perplexed all the people of Bude.

There was **an Old Person of Pinner,**
As thin as a lath, if not thinner;
They dressed him in white,
And roll'd him up tight,
That elastic Old Person of Pinner.

There was **an Old Person of Hurst**,
Who drank when he was not athirst;
When they said, "You'll grow fatter!"
He answered, "What matter?"
That globular Person of Hurst.

There was **an Old Person of Newry,**

Whose manners were tinctured with fury;

He tore all the Rugs,

And broke all the Jugs,

Within twenty miles' distance of Newry.

There was **an Old Man of Marseilles**,

Whose daughters wore bottle-green veils;

They caught several fish,

Which they put in a dish,

And sent to their Pa at Marseilles.

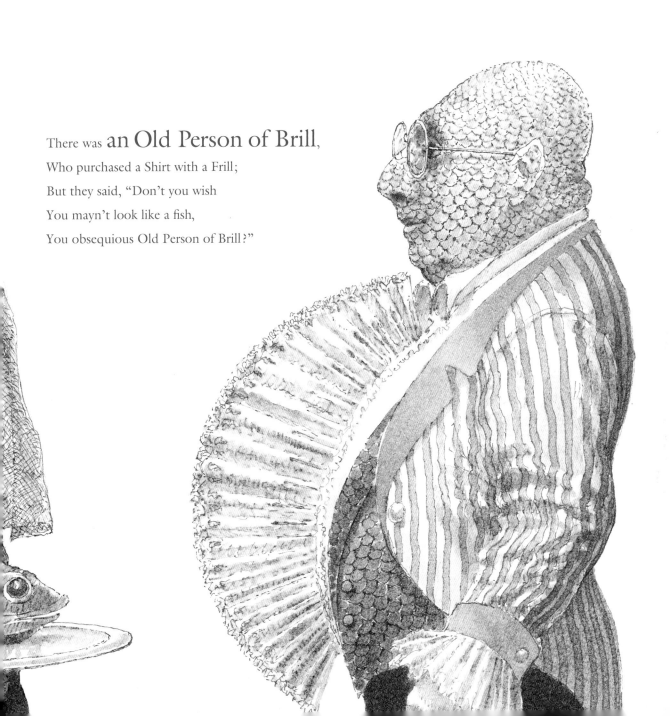

There was **an Old Person of Brill**,

Who purchased a Shirt with a Frill;

But they said, "Don't you wish

You mayn't look like a fish,

You obsequious Old Person of Brill?"

There was **an Old Person of Gretna**,

Who rushed down the crater of Etna;

When they said, "Is it hot?"

He replied, "No, it's not!"

That mendacious Old Person of Gretna.

There was **an Old Person of Philæ**,

Whose conduct was dubious and wily;

He rushed up a palm

When the weather was calm,

And observed all the ruins of Philæ.

There was **an Old Man**,
who when little

Fell casually into a Kettle;

But, growing too stout,

He could never get out,

So he passed all his life in that Kettle.

There was **an Old Person of Mold**,

Who shrank from sensations of cold;

So he purchased some muffs,

Some furs, and some fluffs,

And wrapped himself up from the cold.

There was **a Young Lady whose bonnet**

Came untied when the birds sat upon it;

But she said, "I don't care!

All the birds in the air

Are welcome to sit on my bonnet!"

There was an Old Man on whose nose,

Most birds of the air could repose;

But they all flew away

At the closing of day,

Which relieved that Old Man and his nose.

Edward Lear (1812–1888)

There was an Old Derry down Derry,
Who loved to make little folks merry;
So he wrote them a book
And with laughter they shook
At the fun of the Derry down Derry.

Born in London in 1812, Edward Lear was the youngest of fifteen children. When their father was sent to debtors prison, Lear's elder sister, Anne, raised him. Under her instruction he discovered his natural talent for art, creating careful studies of flowers, butterflies, birds, and animals.

By the time he was eighteen, Lear was the one giving art lessons. And when the Royal Zoological Society commissioned him to draw the parrots in the Regent's Park Zoo, the resulting portfolio of forty-two lithographs was so well received that some compared Lear's talent favorably to Audubon's. Lear went on to illustrate more of the zoo's inhabitants, including monkeys, reptiles, and owls. In 1832, Lord Stanley, the son of the twelfth Earl of Derby, asked Lear to come to the Earl's Knowsley residence to paint the family's menagerie. The Earl's grandchildren delighted in the artist's presence. Lear—calling himself Derry down Derry—entertained them by inventing nonsense verses about curious old men, eccentric young women, and the exploits of the menagerie, illustrating each with his lively caricatures.

When A BOOK OF NONSENSE was first published in 1846, it did not bear Lear's name. Believing the whimsical book might damage his reputation as a sober-minded naturalist and landscape painter, Lear used the pen name "Derry down Derry." A BOOK OF NONSENSE was an immediate success—appealing to children and adults alike—so, of course, Lear's name went on the second edition. Soon he was showing doubting strangers the name sewn in his hat to prove that Edward Lear was a man and not just a name.

James Wines

James Wines is an internationally known artist and architect who began his career as a sculptor, but gradually expanded the scope of his art to include the design of buildings, landscapes, and public spaces. In 1970, he co-founded the New York-based architectural firm of SITE Projects with three other artists, of whom only Michelle Stone remains a partner. As president of SITE, Wines heads an interdisciplinary team, creating architecture in response to social and environmental concerns. The firm's more recent work addresses how buildings can be integrated into the natural environment.

Wines sees architecture as a set of recycled archetypes. SITE's early work dealt with reinterpreting images of the American highway, redefining certain buildings—such as warehouses—that ordinarily melt into their surroundings or recede into our subconscious because they are so common. In the 1970s, for example, Best Products Company, the nationwide chain of catalog showrooms, agreed to let SITE experiment with the shape and structure of the ubiquitous showroom. The firm's resulting designs challenged every expectation and preconception of what a merchandise mart should look like. The facade of one showroom in Virginia peeled away from the building; in Texas, another crumbled into a pile of rubble. In Maryland, one end of a facade lifted up off its foundation; a forest grew between the front doors and the lobby of a Best in Virginia.

Playful, fanciful, at times surreal, Wines' designs capture the imaginations of all who view them. His fascination with the many-layered meanings of architecture make him the ideal reinterpreter of Edward Lear's Nonsense. "Lear's verse is quite relevant to our world, full of chaos and uncertainty," he says. "On one hand you can interpret the limericks as dark, perverse, or irreverent commentaries. But remember, he created them for children. And our world is so desperately in need of the humanistic warmth and humor that is at the heart of these classics."

BEST FOREST BUILDING
Richmond, Virginia
1980

There was a Young Lady Most Dear,
Who brought me love, humor and cheer;
In thanks to my Kriz,
I dedicate this,
Book of Nonsense by Old Edward Lear.
—JW